D1312423

INSTRUCTIONS
PLEASE READ THIS FIRST

The story of Sam the Sleepy Sheep has been specially designed to help make it easy for children to drift off into a natural, deep sleep.

This book works using highly effective sleep-inducing language patterns (included throughout the story). Some words and phrases might seem a little "out of place" or repetitive, but every single word in Sam the Sleepy Sheep is included on purpose. By adding, removing or changing words, you could make the story much less effective, as such, you will get the very best results if you **read the story exactly as it is written** (that goes for punctuation too – everything's there for a reason).

It can be a really good idea to read the story to yourself (out loud) a couple of times before you read it to "an audience". By doing this, you will familiarise yourself with the story, and learn how to read it most effectively by using the simple instructions provided here.

**Note: If you find it too tricky to read yourself,
Sam the Sleepy Sheep is also available as an audio book.**

For best results, children should be lying down to listen to the story, rather than sitting up and helping to turn the pages/look at the pictures (it's not essential, but it definitely helps get them to sleep easier). Also, before you read the story, always try and make sure that you won't be interrupted whilst reading.

Please be aware that some children might need to hear Sam the Sleepy Sheep a couple of times before they can relax completely – please do remember, a brand new book can be exciting for children, and it's hard to be excited AND relaxed at the same time. So whatever happens, **please stick with it!**

When reading the story, it's important that you take your time, because even though the story is quite long, trying to read through it quickly will reduce its effectiveness. Also, as you read, attempt to make your voice as soft, soothing and relaxing as possible, but not monotonous and boring.

Throughout the book, you will notice certain words/phrases are emphasised in 3 different ways. Here's what they all mean:

- **Words/phrases in bold are "directions"** – these should be read in a *slightly* different way than the normal text. Use a "downwards-inflection" (lowering the tone of your voice/gradually making your voice go a little deeper) during the bold parts. For example:

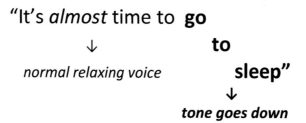

"It's *almost* time to **go**
↓   **to**
normal relaxing voice   **sleep"**
↓
tone goes down

By doing this, you're turning the bold part into a direction, and by reading it in a way that is slightly different to normal (but try not to be *too* obvious), children will generally go along with these directions without even realising it.

You can also **say these words a little slower**, and make the words **feel a little sleepier** using your voice as best you can.

- Words in red give you an option – these are only used when referring to the reader (you), and they are only used twice. They will say one of two things...

  The first will say; mummy/daddy, referring to the person who is reading the story (you). However:

  - if you're not the child's parent...
  - if the child refers to you by another name...
  - if you'd prefer to use a different title (i.e. mommy/mom/ma)...

  ...then you can substitute mummy/daddy for a title/name that fits your own personal situation better.

  The second will say; mummy /& daddy, so if you're a single parent, you have the option to omit the parent that isn't you (if you want to).

- *Words in purple are instructions for YOU* – this means you should follow the instructions suggested. There are 3 different instructions, which are to *YAWN* to *BREATHE IN/OUT* or to *PRETEND TO SPRINKLE SLEEPING POWDER OVER YOUR CHILDS HEAD*.

  If you feel that the last instruction (sprinkling powder) might be too visually stimulating, feel free to leave it out.

Extra reading tips:

- Even though the story lets you know when to *YAWN* whilst reading, you can always add a few more yawns if you like... (try not to yawn *too* much though – a little yawning goes a long way).

- You can also yawn whilst saying words/names (so long as they can still be understood).

- If you see 3 dots … it means you should pause. I.e. stop talking for a moment longer than you normally would, this helps to emphasise certain words and phrases.

- OPTIONAL EXTRA – You can occasionally add in the words; **"that's right"** whenever you see your child close their eyes, get comfortable or relax. This will help them to continue to do just that. **"That's right"** should be said in the same way as all the other **bold parts**.

...now it's time for bed,
and time to go to sleep...

...so here's your sleepy
bedtime friend...

Sam the Sleepy Sheep

by Rory Z Fulcher & Dr. Kate Beaven-Marks

Sam the **Sleepy** Sheep had had a wonderful day with his family and friends, but now it was getting late, and *almost* time to ... **go to sleep ...** Now, Sam was exactly as old as you are, and loved to do all of the things that *you* do ... Playing with toys and having fun, and so, after putting on his pyjamas and playing for a little while, his mummy said;

"You look like ... **you're getting a little bit sleepy ... your eyes are getting heavy and tired ...**" and that it would soon be time for Sam to ... **go to sleep ... Now**, even though Sam could feel his ... **eyes getting really tired ...** he *thought* he was having too much fun, and that he wasn't quite ready to ... **feel so tired and go to sleep now ...** because he didn't want to miss out on anything, by ... **easily drifting off to sleep ... with every breath, and every thought, helping to relax even more now ...**

Sometimes, even if Sam was ... **becoming more and more tired ...** but he *thought* he wanted to carry on playing, his mummy would let him take a toy to bed which would help him to ... **go to sleep.** Out of all of the toys in Sam's toy box, his very favourite was his fluffy teddy bear named Rupert, who would play with him until he ... **can't even try to keep those eyes open any longer ...** and Sam wondered whether *Rupert* perhaps wanted to ... **close those tired eyes and relax ...** because even bears can ... **begin to feel really sleepy ...** *YAWN* at the end of a long day.

But Sam decided, playing with toys in bed isn't as much fun as playing with them in the morning, after **you can go deeply asleep for a long time**

… because in the morning you'll have more energy to play, and you'll be ready for a whole new day of fun. Just because … **you're going to sleep now …** will make tomorrow arrive that much sooner, and … **going to sleep now …** can actually be a lot more fun, because … **you can begin to sleep and dream …** about all kinds of wonderful, interesting things.

Just by **closing your eyes and going to sleep now … you can dream of anything you wish …** and perhaps tonight as you … **go to sleep and begin to dream …** you might … **find yourself drifting down …** a **peaceful** and **relaxing** stream in a beautiful boat, **floating gently** on a **comfy,** fluffy cloud, or exploring in a … **peacefully dreaming …** magic garden, filled with beautiful plants and wonderful **sleepy …** animals. Completely **safe, secure and relaxed … dreaming happy, wonderful dreams as you're sleeping …** and the quicker … **you can go to sleep …** the more time you have to … **enjoy you're dreaming now,** about anything you like. You may even **dream about dreaming and sleeping now, as you relax.**

Sometimes, Mummy Sheep even let Sam stay up past his bedtime, but when Sam the Sheep stayed up past his bedtime, he'd soon … *YAWN* **get really sleepy …** and wouldn't even be able to keep his **eyes** from **closing,** because … **the more you think about trying not to … close your eyes … the heavier, and more tired they become …** and Sam would always end up … **closing those eyes now, without even thinking about it.** Sam decided that going to bed and … **going to sleep now,** is OK.

So he told his mummy he was ready to get into bed and **… go to sleep …** and as he was **… comfortably relaxing …** in bed, Mummy Sheep said;

"I love you, and you are perfect just the way you are … and your mummy /& daddy will always love you, no matter what." This made Sam happy, and just like you, Sam loves to **… make everybody happy** too, **by going to sleep now …** And so she tucked him in to his **sleepy …** sheepy bed, and she began to **… settle down,** to read him a wonderful, **comfortable, sleepy** bedtime story, kind of like how you are listening to *your* mummy/daddy reading *you* a story as **you are going to sleep now …**

Mummy Sheep told Sam that it's OK if **… you want to fall asleep before the story ends,** and **now …** if you want to, **you can go to sleep even sooner …** because you know this story has a happy ending, and you will be able to **… sleep peacefully now … all night long …** and **the next time you listen to this story, you will be able to … fall asleep … even faster than before …**

Sam snuggled up in bed, and yawned *YAWN* thinking about **… falling asleep now …** and noticed that he was starting to **breathe slowly … and deeply … slowly breathing in …** *BREATHE IN* **… and out …** *BREATHE OUT*

"Before we read the story" Mummy Sheep said "**you can make yourself nice and relaxed,** because **relaxing now** will help you to enjoy the story,

and … **you will easily fall asleep …** when … **you are ready to fall asleep …"** **now,** because Sam knew that mummy was *very* clever, he decided to **listen and relax …**

"**I'd like you to relax your feet and your toes**" said Mummy Sheep "**and now let your legs and your knees relax completely. Relax your tummy all the way to your shoulders … let everything go relaxed and soft … sleepy and heavy. Relax your arms and your neck … so sleepy. Relax your face and your mouth … and relax your heavy, heavy eyes now …"** and as Sam … **let everything relax now,** he began to **feel really good.**

"**Allow your whole body to feel really heavy now … Sink all the way down comfortably into your bed … Drifting deeper and deeper, relaxing more and more *YAWN* … Very tired now … and it doesn't matter if your eyes are open, or you … close them now, because that will help you … relax more**" and as Sam does … **feel completely relaxed …** he just wants to … **go to sleep …** but he thinks he will **try …** to listen to the story for just a little while longer, because he knows he *will* **fall asleep soon …**

And so Mummy Sheep began to **slowwwly** read: Once upon a time, there was a magical toy-maker, and the toy-maker made a magical toy frog named Mr **Sleepy. Now,** Mr **Sleepy** is a very special frog, and the very special thing about Mr **Sleepy** is his voice. His voice is so … **relaxing …** that as he talks, **every word helps you to … feel relaxed from the very top of your head, all the way dowwwwn to the tips of your toes …**

If Mr **Sleepy** were here now, he'd **snuggle up in your bed**, and he would talk to you in his magical **sleepy** voice, until **you can't even remember just what was said … because you are becoming so very relaxed and sleepy … that every other thought may just … drift away now.**

Mr **Sleepy** also yawns a lot, and every time you hear a yawn, **it can help you to become more and more tired,** *YAWN* and so **very relaxed** …

And you can remember to forget to remember everything I just said as you go on relaxing now … because Mr **Sleepy**'s voice, and his **… words are so relaxing …** every time he speaks, he often **… begins to fall asleep** … himself, and he would **… become so very tired …** that he would **completely forget** what he was doing **before** he would **just fall asleep now …** *YAWN*

Mr **Sleepy** would tell **relaxing** stories about all of his friends, who lived in the **… peacefully sleeping …** woods of Dreamland, such as his friend Bobby the Baby Bunny. Bobby was sometimes so busy bouncing, that he completely forgot to **… go to sleep …** So Bobby's mummy would ask Mr **Sleepy** to come and tell Bobby his **sleepy, relaxing** story that helps you **… go to sleep …** Because, **when you hear this story, everyone around starts to feel sleepy** *YAWN* **…** and just by **listening to this story now, you can go to sleep without even thinking about anything …** So, Mr **Sleepy** *did* tell his story in his **relaxing, sleepy** voice … because he loved helping little bouncy bunnies **… go to sleep …**

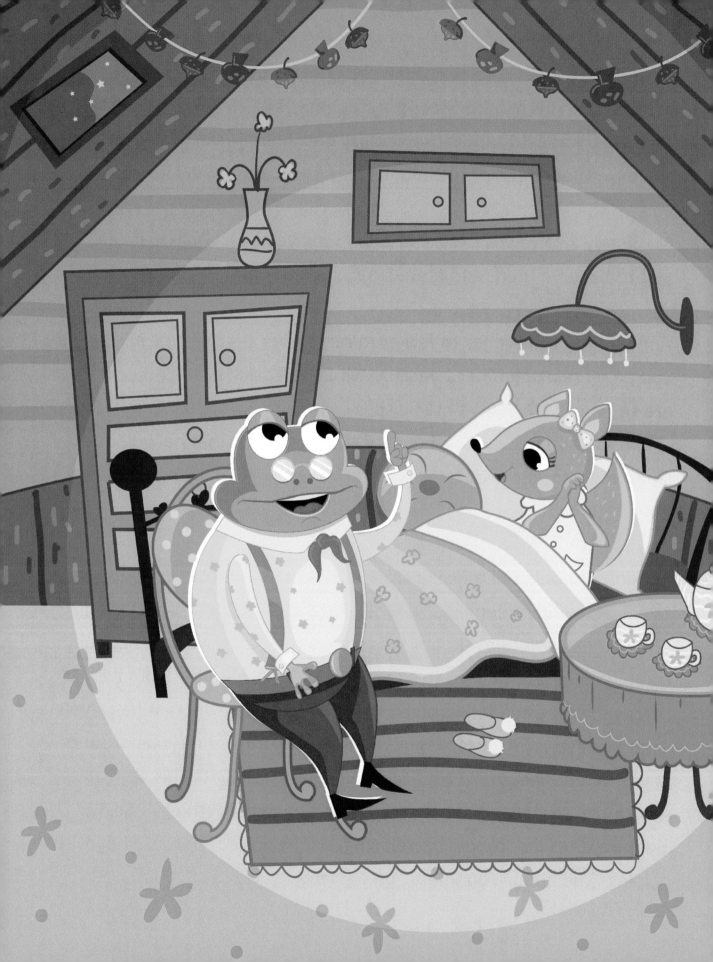

and before very long, Bobby the Baby Bunny would **... completely forget about playing** and bouncing, as his **... eyes are getting so heavy** *YAWN* **becoming so tired ...** he would simply **... relax now, and drift off to sleep.**

After saying goodnight to Mrs Bunny, Mr **Sleepy** was about to go home so he could **... just relax with those tired eyes closed**, when he met his friend Suzy the Squirrel, and she was **... so very tired and sleepy ...**

"Hello Mr **Sleepy**" *YAWN* she yawned, "I **... feel so tired**, and I wish I could just **... go to sleep now ...** Can you please tell me a story to help me **... go to sleep ...** because I have a lot of things to do tomorrow, and your **... stories can always help us relax, and drift off to sleep ... without even needing to try ...**"

Mr **Sleepy** was happy to help, and soon, Suzy the Squirrel got **snuggled up in bed ... safe, warm and comfortable**, and Mr **Sleepy** began to tell another of his wonderful **... going-to-sleep ...** stories. *This time*, the story was about a friendly old wizard. Suzy **closed** her **eyes** and she quickly started to **... fall asleep ...** as Mr **Sleepy** began to **slowwwwly** read:

There once was a wizard who lived in the **sleeping** woods of Dreamland, in a beautiful tree-house made of **comfortable** pillows and **warm, cosy** blankets. Anyone who saw the wizard's house would instantly want to **... go to sleep ...** their **eyes getting heavy and tired**, and they would just **... lay down and drift off to sleep ...** just as **...** *you* **are now going to sleep ...**

because the wizard's house was **so wonderfully calm and relaxed now.**

Deep inside his **sleepy** enchanted tree-house, was a room, and this special room was where the wizard mixed up his magical **eyes-closing** spells and **... falling-asleep ...** potions. It was filled from top to bottom with jars of all sizes and bubbling bowls, **heavy** books, and **floating** glass balls. The wizard liked it when people would **... go to sleep ...** because **going to sleep ...** makes **... you feel good now.** So he decided to make a magical **sleeping** powder that would help anybody to **... easily and quickly go to sleep now, without even thinking about it ...**

The wizard mixed a spoonful of **dreaming** and a dash of **snooze**, into a big bowl full of magical **sleeping** ingredients, and he **quietly** whispered the magic words;

"**Sleepy ... sleepy ... deeply sleepy ...**" and so the magical **... go-to-sleep** powder was made. **Feeling really tired ...** himself, he started to put away his magical tools, and **... almost in a dream now,** he accidentally spilled a little **... go-to-sleep** powder right onto the head of Cecil, his **sleepy** black cat. For the briefest of moments, Cecil wondered what was going on, and sooner than he could **try and think of anything else,** he yaaaawned *YAWN* **... relaxed completely ...** and flopped down on to the rug, **going to sleep now ... all the way dowwwwn ... deep asleep now ...**

And because this **... go-to-sleep** powder is so powerful, the wizard

carefully tucked the powder **dowwwwn, deep** into his special, secret magical pocket, because even just by *imagining* a little **… go-to-sleep** powder being sprinkled over you *PRETEND TO SPRINKLE OVER CHILDS HEAD* … you can **… fall asleep now … and every breath you breathe, is relaxing you more and more …**

So, the wizard made sure Cecil is **… very comfy now**, and then with his **… go-to-sleep** powder tucked away, **safe, secure and comfortable** in his pocket, he left his magical tree-house by sliding down the **sleepy** slide. **Slowwwwly** sliding **down, relaxing more and more …** and into a huge, **relaxing,** fluffy pillow at the bottom **… so comfortably relaxed now …**

He then **drifted slowly dowwwwn** a nice, calm path, into the **sleeping** woods of Dreamland. On his way through the **… peacefully sleeping …** woods, with **… everything still and quiet now,** the wizard wandered, and as he *wandered,* he *wondered* where he could use his magical **… go-to-sleep** powder. As he was thinking that very thought, he heard a **quiet** rustle beside him, and out of the bush **slowwwwly** appeared Bertie the Badger and his brother, Barry. They were both **… very, very tired.**

"What are you doing, Mr Wizard?" the **tired** badgers asked … and the wizard said; "I've just invented something *very special* and **sleepy** …"

"We'd love to find out more" said the badgers "but it's almost time for us to **… go to sleep,** because we're **… getting really tired now.**" *YAWN*

"I can help you with **… going to sleep now …**" said the wizard, and he reached **deep, deep dowwwwn …** into his pocket, pulled out his magical **… go-to-sleep** powder, and **softly** sprinkled it over Bertie and Barry. The badger brothers **swayed gently … rocking peacefully from side to side … rocking and relaxing, and getting more and more sleepy with every breath …** until they both sllllllumped down onto the **comfy, cosy** grass, and began to snore. **Deep asleep now … Deep asleep …**

The wizard **slowly drifted** away **dowwwwn** the path, further into the **… peacefully sleeping …** woods of Dreamland, delighted with how well his magical **… go-to-sleep** powder had helped Bertie and Barry to **… fall asleep …** just as *you* can easily **relax, and dream of going to sleep now …**

"I wonder who else wants to **… go to sleep …**" the wizard thought.

A little further along the path, it was *really* **… becoming sleepy …** and dark. The wizard saw a **… very tired …** old man sitting **comfortably** on a big wooden bench, listening to the wonderful **sleepy** sounds of the woods, and **… relaxing with every sound … relaxing more and more … deeper and deeper …** but the old man just couldn't quite **… get to sleep now …** The friendly wizard said hello to the old man, and as he did so, he took his powerful **… go-to-sleep** powder from **deep, deep dowwwwn** in his pocket, and sprinkled just a little over the **…very tired …** old man.

And as he watched him **… breathe in relaxation, and breathe out …**

and relax even more, the old man quickly began to **... fall deep, deep asleep ... with every breath, getting even sleepier ...** and as he and **you can easily fall asleep**, we can also **... feel happy, safe and so comfortably relaxed now ...**

The wizard smiled a happy smile, sat down on the bench next to the old man, who was **... now deeply asleep, and feeling good ...** and the wizard decided, that after helping everyone else **... go to sleep ...** it was about time for him to **... fall asleep now ...** as well. So he reached **deep, deep dowwwwn** into his pocket, poured a biiiig handful of his **... go-to-sleep** powder, and gently sprinkled it over *himself* **... drifting off into a wonderful, deep sleep now ... every breath, relaxing ... every sound, relaxing ... every thought, relaxing. Sleeping deeper and deeper ... more and more comfortable now.**

When Mr **Sleepy** the frog finished telling the story about the magical wizard and his **... go-to-sleep** powder, Suzy the Squirrel was past **going to sleep**, in fact she was already **... deep, deep asleep,** and will **... stay fast asleep until tomorrow morning ...** but Mr **Sleepy** had **... become so sleepy and tired ...** himself, that he would have to **slowwwwly** walk home.

Even **... thinking about every step makes you more and more tired,** he thought. But eventually Mr **Sleepy** arrived home, and he was **... so, so tired now ...** that he couldn't stop his **heavy eyes** from **closing.**

So he **settled down** into his nice warm bed, yaaawning *YAWN* and **snuggled up, nice and comfy ...** then Mr **Sleepy** would ... **simply fall asleep ... deep, deep asleep ...** and just as *he* can ... **go to sleep now**, so *you* can sleep just as well ... **completely relaxed ... so comfortable now ... and tomorrow you can fall asleep even faster than the day after yesterday, now ...**

Finally, with a yaaaawn *YAWN* ... Mummy Sheep finished reading the story of Mr **Sleepy,** and Sam was ... **sleeping now, and dreaming now ... Deep, deep asleep ... all comfy and cuddled up in bed ...** So she closed the book **quietly** and turned off the light, and Sam would ... **sleep deeply all night long, and dream wonderful, happy dreams ... Comfortable and safe ... and deep, deep asleep now ...**

And just like Sam the **Sleepy** Sheep, now it's time to ... **go to sleep.**

Goodnight!

About the Authors

Rory Z Fulcher   **Dr. Kate Beaven-Marks**

Based in the UK, **Rory Z Fulcher** and **Dr. Kate Beaven-Marks** have extensive experience with helping people of all ages to go to sleep.

Rory and Kate are experts in using stories and metaphors to help people make positive changes, and are highly trained in Communication, Hypnotherapy, and Neuro-Linguistic Programming (NLP).

They are both principal trainers for The Hypnotherapy Training Company (www.HypnoTC.com)

Made in the USA
Middletown, DE
24 August 2022

72206728R00020